The Triple-Soy Decaf-Latte Era

How Business and Organization are Fundamentally Transforming

Alpesh M. Bhatt

The Five Transformations

Setting Context

For the past two decades, organizations have been grasping for ways to deal with the alarming rate of change they are experiencing, both internally and in the marketplace. We have developed countless methods for managing change and, despite a completely abysmal record of results, we continue to fail to see that the issue is not one of method but of mindset. There is no 'right way' to manage change because change cannot be managed... at least not the kind of change that corporate executives are losing sleep over.

This brief book is not a how-to; it contains no answers and, despite there being five discreet elements to consider, offers no real prescription to follow. If you are in business in the early days of the 21st century, answers and prescriptions are not what you need.

What you may instead need, what may be of greatest benefit if you are to thrive in the world that is emerging, is to become aware of the set of assumptions and biases that form the deep background against which you see the world of work. In our experience, examining these assumptions consciously will allow you to reenter your world with an understanding of the fundamental shifts in mindset that need to occur in order for you to deal with the things that currently show up for you and your organization as 'problems'.

The Five Transformations in its written form is a weak substitute for a real conversation, but I've found that it is enough to get the work started for you. Use this little book as a set of provocations, as a series of conversations to start with your peers and your employees and, perhaps even your customers, clients, vendors, and the communities in which you operate.

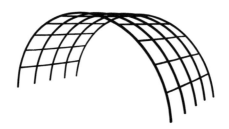

Punctuated Equilibrium

Change Isn't What You Think It Is

Most people think of evolution as something along the line of 'gradual progress over time'. The way evolution actually works however is through the concept of 'punctuated equilibrium'...

Instead of a slow, continuous movement, evolution tends to be characterized by long periods of virtual standstill ("equilibrium"), that are "punctuated" by episodes of very fast development of new forms.

(Stephen Jay Gould and Niles Eldredge)

There are three important things to note about this understanding of evolution:

During those **'long periods of virtual standstill'**, there is actually a lot of change going on. But it is change that is about constantly reestablishing equilibrium or a balanced state. A simple example would be that, over a series of generations wolf packs develop better hearing, making them better hunters. However, at the same time – or perhaps only slightly later – the deer population that the wolves prey on develops longer legs, thereby making them better able to escape the wolves. The important thing to note here is that if we look at either the wolves or the deer in isolation, we would say that a lot has changed. But when we look at the ecosystem between the two, we see that there is relative balance – equilibrium – in the system and not much has really changed at all.

Extending this to our economic lives, for most of our history when we look at single organizations or single industries in isolation, it seems that there is a lot of change happening. In reality, within the broader economic system, there is a relative equilibrium. We have what I call the **Red Queen Effect:** organizations keep changing in a never-ending race simply to sustain their current level of fitness. This keeps the consultants busy and, in fact, is necessary work; the alternate is to not maintain the current level of fitness relative to the marketplace and therefore die a slow death.

During those rare **'episodes of very fast development of new forms'**, almost all existing species become extinct. At this risk of oversimplifying the situation, the fundamental environmental conditions change and, given the fact that most species were designed to succeed by playing some niche role in the existing environment, they quickly die out. Think dinosaurs in the days after the asteroid hit: massive, cold-blooded reptiles that evolved over a long period of time through Red Queen-type change that suddenly found themselves in an environment where the amount of sunlight available to warm their blood had been dramatically reduced by the pervasive dust clouds raised by the asteroid. Within a very short period of time in geological terms these species simply died off, **completely incapable of surviving in the new ecosystem**. And in their place, new species - marginal players in the old ecosystem – suddenly find the conditions perfect for flourishing.

In our economic lives, the last 'punctuation' was the revolution that was catalyzed by Gutten-berg's printing press and culminated in what we call the Industrial Era. Prior to the Industrial Era, the dominant 'economic species' were those that thrived in an ecosystem defined by Land, Monarchy and Church. Without digging into the details of why and how, the point to be made is that over the course of a relatively short period of time, those 'species' died out completely and a totally different set of species – Capitalists – emerged, finding that the new ecosystem suited them perfectly. (Those we would come to call 'capitalists' existed prior to the Industrial Era, but they were a marginal species as the economic ecosystem prior to Industrialization did not provide the elements they needed to thrive).

During periods of 'punctuation', when the fundamentals of the ecosystem have changed, most of what worked in the past and most of what you know is not going to be valued. In fact, everything you know for certain is a source of massive risk because **what you know is relative to a reality that no longer exists.**

During a period of Punctuation, a species' instinct is to engage in Red Queen work – get better, do more, improve, and above all else: manage the changes that are going on. But it is this very instinct that will prevent the species from surviving. What is required now is not doing more or better relative to the known world, but a **willingness to learn the nature of the new world and engage in completely redesigning oneself to thrive in that environment.**

For the first time in 300+ years, we are in the midst of a Punctuation. The fundamentals of our economic ecosystem are shifting.

This is NOT about the financial crisis, the mortgage crisis, or any other crisis or event. Those events, as significant and painful as they may be, are symptoms at best.

The asteroid that has hit our economic ecosystem is **Access.**

Access to markets.
Access to capital.
Access to technology.
Access to each other.

Access is rapidly undermining the economic advantage of scale, size, efficiency and, ultimately, organization as we know it.

In each of the next five sections, we will look at a fundamental transformation that has taken place in our economic ecosystem as a result of **Access**.

Make/Sell

The answer seems obvious if we are responding from the background assumptions of the Industrial Era, right? They make stuff. Or more specifically, they take raw material and make something to sell to a market: Nike takes nylon, cotton, and rubber to make a shoe; Starbucks takes coffee beans and water to make coffee; Toyota takes steel, rubber, plastic, and electronics to make a car. Businesses exist because they have something that they can make and sell to us to produce a profit. But a big challenge with this is that by emphasizing the product or service, you emphasize the transactions around that product or service and habituate your customers to a strictly transactional relationship with you. This is fine if the nature of your product/service is so specialized, so rare, that the customer cannot go anywhere else. But guess what? In the world that's emerging, there will always be somewhere else your customer can go. I don't care how specialized your product is, how competition-proof your service seems, somewhere out there a guy in a garage is doing something that will spin your business out of control in the very near future.

Sense/Respond

Don't worry, companies will still need to make things in order to exist, but as business is transforming, that is just the price of admission and has nothing to do with "what the organization does." So yes, with industrial assumptions, Starbucks makes coffee– but that is not the business they are in. And... someone ought to tell Dunkin Donuts.

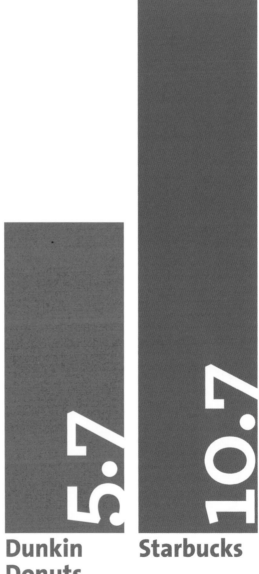

Dunkin Donuts   **Starbucks**

Total Revenue (billions) 2010

According to a national taste test, more Americans preferred Dunkin' Donuts coffee over Starbucks. Yet, Starbucks – bumps in the road during the mid-2000's aside – is a more successful organization. That's because Starbucks' insight was not that the world needed a perfect low-fat, white chocolate mocha espresso, but rather that we needed our third place. Huh? OK, consider this:

If you live in England or Ireland, you have work and you have home, and then you also have... your local pub (not just any pub, your local pub). In continental Europe, you have your café; in India, you have your local tea stall. The point is that, as human beings, we have always had this 'third place'. When we were hunters we had our economic life in the jungle, we had our home life in our hut or cave and we had our third place around the communal fire where we told stories and sang songs. It is fundamentally human to have a third place...and yet, as a nation, we have become nomads: we change jobs every 3.5 years and move homes every 7 years. And so we no longer join Elks Clubs, 4H's, etc., and we aren't involved in our churches in the same way as we used to be. We've lost our third place.

This is the business Starbucks is really in: to be our third place. Starbucks has their stores packed with customers at tables who are getting work done, catching up with friends, or reading books. Dunkin' Donuts has lines at their drive-thru windows packed with customers participating in transactions. Run this little experiment: go into a Dunkin Donuts and bring in your food AND a cup of coffee from somewhere else. Sit down at a table, start enjoying your food and watch the reaction you get from the staff. Then go do the same thing at Starbucks. I've run this experiment, multiple times. Employees at Starbucks stores won't mind because you're actually engaging them in the business they're in: being your third place. The employees themselves may not even be familiar with this phrase, but it's embedded in their culture.

Don't be confused here - making a good product or providing a quality service is very necessary for a company to exist, but it is just the price of admission. The real game in the new ecosystem is, what is the meaning you create for people? More accurately, what is the possibility you open up for them? Starbucks doesn't need to have the best-tasting coffee because it is simply not the business they're in.

First & Best Answer

Cost, speed, and quality are the drivers of competition in the Industrial Era. This is Management 101 stuff: you win the game by being the cheapest, providing the product/service the fastest, or by providing the highest quality in your industry (and you can have two of those three if you'd like but only at the expense of the third: you can be cheapest AND fastest but quality will be terrible, you can be fastest AND highest quality but cost will be very high, etc.).

Take a close look at your marketing campaigns, at your key organizational initiatives, at your employee compensation systems-- they all reinforce one of the three Industrial Era competition drivers.

On-Demand

No, a company can't have an over-priced, poor quality product that takes twice as long to get to market as their competitor, but these three elements of competition are merely the price of admission to play the game. The emerging ecosystem requires that you engage at a totally different level.

Remember playing with Lego's? What I remember is that you went to the store, picked up either a box for a specific model or a box with a collection of general Lego pieces (and there were never enough of those wheels!). Go to the Lego website and download the DesignByMe software. You now have access to a digital version of every piece Lego makes, and every time you open the software, it updates your collection with any new pieces that have become available. Start with a blank slate and get creative, create or load one of their many pre-existing models and start customizing. When you're done, click a button that will take you to their website to place an order. Cool! A customized Lego set, right? Oh, but it gets so much better.

Once your kit is priced (you pay the same on a per-piece basis as you would if you were buying an off-the-shelf kit), you get to design the box that the logos will come in! Upload a picture of your child and create a customized Lego box with a special birthday message. And then, you can even customize the instruction sheet that will be placed inside of the box.

This isn't faster, this isn't cheaper, and this isn't best quality. This is something totally different; it is 'on-demand'. It is EXACTLY what you want, when you want it, how you want it. I call this the Triple-Soy-Decaf-Latte Phenomena and it defines how human beings in the emerging economy expect to deal with EVERYTHING.

There are too many examples of this to mention (and many, many more are showing up daily), but I'll leave you with one more: Toyota released a new automobile product line several years ago called Scion. Go do a quick bit of research and you will quickly learn that Toyota designed this line of cars to be completely customizable, to be a car that you could quickly turn into your own one-of-a-kind. In other words, the Scion is the world's first Triple-Soy-Decaf-Latte automobile brand. And, even in an industry that one might think couldn't possibly deal with customers in an on-demand way, it is only the beginning.

The issue to really pay attention to here is that, in the emerging ecosystem, you MUST enable individual expression. Choice is no longer enough, everything you offer must be on-demand. Lego, Toyota, Nike (check out the NIKEiD sneakers) and many others are in the early stages of learning how to generate value by giving customers the opportunity to create exactly what they want, when they want it.

Tangible

There are two types of capital that are critical to an Industrial Era business: Material and Financial. Material Capital is all of the raw materials required to create the product or service that the organization makes and sells. Financial Capital is the cash and credit required to ensure a steady flow of Material Capital.

I can hear you asking, what about the employees? In the industrial mindset, employees are Material Capital; they are a specific form of machinery purchased to perform certain specialized tasks. They have a spec sheet—also known as a resume. We evaluate them and calibrate their performance on the same quarterly and annual cycle as we do industrial and digital machinery.

My intention here is not to be cynical but to underscore the design of the game: our model of organization was created when 99% of the work force did highly repetitive, relatively simple tasks and it simply has not changed much since then. We have certainly become much more humanistic in our approach and, in my experience, the vast majority of managers are genuinely concerned with their employees' wellbeing. **However, at the level of organizational design, it cannot be denied that we conceive of the human being as a form of material capital.**

Intangible

As with the other Transformations, the forms of capital of the Industrial Era – financial and material – cannot be ignored; however, in and of themselves, they are insufficient. At least two other forms of capital are critical in the ecosystem that is emerging: Reputational and Social.

Consider Coca-Cola: if you totaled up all of their financial and material capital, it would be worth about $7B. The value of their Reputational Capital? A little over TEN TIMES that. An overly simplified example perhaps but the point holds: The vast majority of their value as an organization is based on something totally intangible. The vast majority of their wealth can't be stored in a bank, can't be put on display in the lobby of corporate headquarters, can't be managed in anywhere near the same manner as their tangible capital (financial and material).

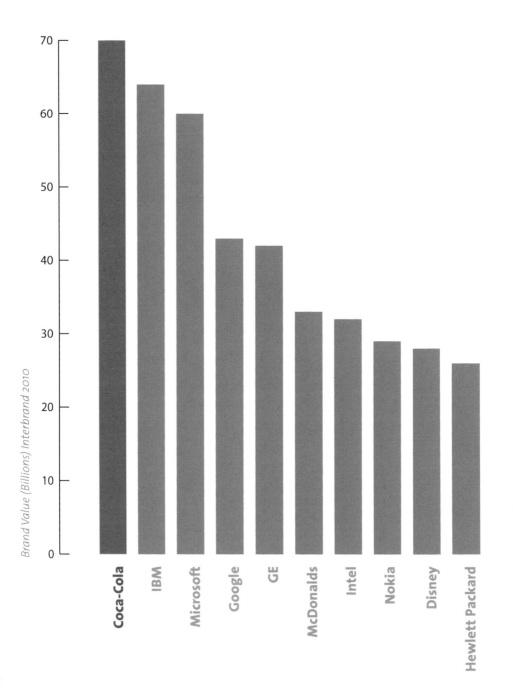

Brand Value (Billions) Interbrand 2010

Coca-Cola	70
IBM	64
Microsoft	60
Google	43
GE	42
McDonalds	33
Intel	32
Nokia	29
Disney	28
Hewlett Packard	26

Consider also the concept of Social Capital, a close cousin to Reputational Capital. The word 'Social' is thrown around a lot these days. Let me provide a simple perspective on this:

Your Social Capital within a network of relationships is the degree to which what you say is actually heard, believed and valued...and proactively carried to others.

Consider your Social Capital with your customers, or how about your employees? Pretty dark thought, isn't it? And if it's not, I'd humbly suggest that you're likely kidding yourself. The reality is that you very likely 'communicate' *to* your customers and your employees. You create messages that contain exactly the perfect articulation of what you want said and then you find just the right channel to drop the message into. This approach does not build Social Capital. In the Industrial Era, this approach built what it was intended to: clear, consistent positioning of a product or service, a fixed identity that others had no real way to challenge or even contribute to. In the post-Industrial Era, the Access era, this approach builds cynicism and distrust.

We no longer want to be spoken to, we demand to be spoken with.

(The clearest articulation of this is contained in a book from 1999, The Cluetrain Manifesto. If you have any involvement in the Marketing function of your organization, this book will be invaluable to you in the emerging ecosystem.)

Note that Social Capital is also completely intangible; it's not a 'thing' but a type of engagement; or more accurately, it is what emerges from a certain type of engagement. This then is the real point about the nature of capital in the ecosystem that is emerging:

The forms of capital that matter most now are those that can only be managed indirectly and that are the product of legitimate, two-way interaction and dialogue with your customers and your employees.

Hierarchical
Centralized Decision-Making
Competition

Given the answers to what an organization does and how it competes in the Industrial Era, it is quite natural that the design of organization be oriented towards hierarchy and centralized decision-making.

This model of organization maximizes the possibility of a high level of control and predictability relative to the 'Make-Sell' purpose of Industrial-Era businesses. In fact, all of Management Science and its sister disciplines such as Industrial Psychology are oriented towards the creation of a high level of control and predictability in service of the decisions made at the top of the hierarchy. In the context of the ecosystem that existed when these disciplines were formed, this not only made sense, it was of enormous value.

Cellular Decentralized Decision-Making Mass Collaboration

In the emerging ecosystem however, there's something to be learned from the phenomenon of "slugging". Slugging is a unique form of commuting also known as "Instant Carpooling" or "Casual Carpooling" where people carpool with complete strangers in order to ride in the high-occupancy lane to downtown Washington DC.

There are a number of unofficial, unmarked pick-up and drop-off locations and nearly 35,000 people participate in this phenomenon on a weekly basis. There has never been a report of a single crime committed by a rider or a driver and there is never money exchanged for the rides. And nobody organized it. There is no city department that conceived this, the concept has no committee, they're not insured, and there is no leader. This is pure mass collaboration creating enormous value. Oh, and you can "slug" to get to downtown DC faster than any method of public transportation. Imagine if the city government had tried to set this up, armed with committees, plans, budgets and consultants?

A more practical reference point for business managers is Whole Foods where, instead of having corporate hiring managers determine who gets hired, the respective local departments make the decision. Instead of having the director of marketing dictate what is on sale and on display at a local meat department, the local meat department decides. Whole Foods sets the broadest possible boundaries to provide space for employees to sense and respond to customer needs in the context of the real business that they are in (to reestablish the intimate and sacred relationship human beings have with their food).

Centralized decision-making simply doesn't make sense when you think of your business the way a Starbucks or a Whole Foods does. Their mindset is: Go make mistakes and learn from them. But this works only if every employee is actually aware of what business they are in AND they are in legitimate engagement – remember Social Capital – between organization and employee.

I know, I know. The nature of Starbucks' and Whole Foods' business requires that their employees be in contact with customers constantly, so this whole decentralized decision-making thing makes more sense and is easier to see the value of. But consider W.L. Gore, a chemical and manufacturing firm. If you are fortunate enough to go to work at Gore, your first 6 months are spent 'wandering' until you find a team or project that excites you. And to whom do you report on that team? You report to the person with the title of "leader" (the only title in the company other than 'associate'). How did that person get the title of leader? The others on the team felt that he/she was best qualified to be leader based upon the phase of the project they were in at the time and they elect a new leader if and when the project priorities change.

I often compare our organizational structure to a democracy to explain the tradeoffs in a structure like ours," she says. "When you look at it from a purely objective standpoint, a democratic government may not be the most time- or cost-effective way to run a country. In the end, however, the quality of life is far better than what you'll find in a dictatorship. **We believe the associate satisfaction and spirit of innovation that result from our culture more than compensate for its challenges.**

- Sally Gore, HR Leader, W.L. Gore

Note the highlight in that quote. If you are a business manager, 'innovation' is a fairly consistent priority for you. As we stated in the introduction to this book, the challenge is that while we are focusing very heavily on innovation in our business today, we are focusing on it with an Industrial Era mindset. We are trying to control innovation as a piece of tangible capital, which it is not. Innovation emerges - like Trust, Loyalty, Reputation, and other forms of intangible capital – as a by-product of dynamic engagement and commitment.

Centralized hierarchies were designed specifically to eliminate innovation in favor of efficient, repeatable, predictable behavior from every employee in the organization. How is it possible that we expect innovation to occur at the levels we need it to while also expecting that we can hold on to a hierarchical view of the organization?

What is needed is an understanding of organization that is Cellular. Each individual work unit must operate with the same autonomy – AND accountability – as a cell in your body does. Imagine if one of your liver cells had to get approval from somewhere up the hierarchy or refer to a job description every time it had a new, unknown toxin to filter out of your bloodstream; you'd be dead tomorrow. That liver cell is a self-contained entity that reacts and interacts with its environment in a completely sense and respond manner. And it is also a part of the whole; it has broad boundaries within which it operates that keep it aligned with the interests of your entire body.

Hard Boundaries
Dialogue
Conquest

The final transformation is perhaps the most challenging for business managers because it pokes at a fundamental question: who really owns and runs your company?

The game as it was designed in the Industrial Era was that the organization had very hard boundaries with its environment. Customers are over here, vendors over there, partners over there, etc. Certain people within the company can speak to certain people outside of the company, but to no one else, and they can only speak about certain things. For example, Customer Service and Sales employees can both speak with customers but about very different things, and there is a mandate against engaging in conversations that you aren't entitled to have. Conversations between the organization and others aren't really conversations at all; they are scripted, rule-bound transactions.

In fact, this dynamic even exists within the organization in the way that different functions interact with each other. The Industrial Era orientation here is, as we have seen in previous transformations, one of control and predictability: 'If we let just anyone in the company talk to customers, it'll be chaos. We won't know if what they're saying is right'.

Permeable Boundaries
Conversation
Co-Creation

If you remember nothing else about the emerging ecosystem, remember this: it's a conversation, not a message. A message seeks to fill all the available space and squeeze out anything that competes with it. The whole point of real conversation is to create new space, to open up possibilities that a single individual – or organization – could not have created on their own.

The degree to which you are willing to facilitate real conversations within your organization and between your organization and it's environment - the degree to which you get that you are your conversational environment - is the degree to which you can seize the opportunities that the new ecosystem provides.

And if you can't – or won't - there are lots of little species of economic animal that naturally operate this way and they are more than happy to take over little parts of your marketplace for you.

DailyBooth

Appl

Bebo

Hi5 **5** Ning

Microsoft

LOCATION BASIN

Mayor Island

NOKIA

UNION OF SOCIAL NETWORKS

in

STREAMS OF ACTIVITY

LAND OF IDENTITY

Social Dis

ID ClaimID

W Wordpress

r Resilient Networks

me About.me

N Namesake

The wonderful cartography from the folks at the Web 2.0 Expo demonstrates the assumptions of the Industrial Era perfectly. It's all about hard boundaries and conquest: 'if I get more, you must get less'. The map suggests that we play with what is on the table; that we play in a zero-sum game. Conquest based upon a zero-sum gain understanding of the world is a blind spot in the emerging ecosystem. In response to the map displayed at the Web 2.0 Expo, the CEO of Facebook commented that:

"Your map's wrong. I think that the biggest part of the map has got to be the uncharted territory. Right? One of the best things about the technology industry is that it's not zero-sum. This thing makes it seem like it's zero-sum. Right? In order to take territory you have to be taking territory from someone else. But I think one of the best things is, we're building real value in the world, not just taking value from other companies."

This is the mindset that the emerging marketplace demands... and not just in the technology industry. In every sector, the emerging reality seems to be 'innovate or die'. But if you teach your organization to think of the game as zero-sum and if you teach it to shut down to legitimate conversation with itself and its marketplace, it will never learn how to truly innovate.

What Sits in the Background

Assumptions of the Industrial and Emerging Eras

We promised you a view of the fundamental shifts that are taking place in the very nature of business and organization. The Five Transformations provide the general themes and we could devote an entire book to each of them if our interest were to provide an exhaustive study, which of course it is not.

Before ending here, however, I'd like to provide one more filter; a somewhat deeper one that provides insight into why you or others may find the Five Transformations difficult to 'believe' or impractical to implement.

The following is a set of 'background assumptions', filters on the world that have us see in a certain way. For each, an alternate filter is offered that, if adopted, would create more possibility in terms of engaging with the Five Transformations.

The world consists of transactions

Our fundamental engagement with the world, in practically every practice area and academic discipline, proceeds from the assumption that the world consists of individual agents that transact with each other. Whether it is a biologist looking at the interaction between two cells or a marketer looking at the interaction between a message and a group of consumers, our primary filter is one of transactions.

The world is understood through cause & effect

If we didn't fundamentally assume that everything is governed by cause and effect, much of what we do in industrial organizations would make no sense. For example, of what use would market research be if we didn't believe that buying behavior is governed by some set of cause and effect chains? Find the right cause/effect chains and you can create the 'causes' that will result in the consumer 'effect' you desire. Similarly, of what use would Performance Management, Culture Surveys, Succession Planning and a hundred other organizational practices be if we didn't believe that everything can be understood - and controlled - through cause and effect relationships?

The world consists of conversations & relationships

Consider that when two agents interact that a fundamentally different entity emerges. As a simple example: if I play the notes C, E and G on a piano, I recognize them as individual 'musical agents'. However, if I play them at the same time, I do not think about their individual identities, nor do I think that they are somehow interacting or transacting; what I hear is a fundamentally new thing with it's own identity: a chord.

Imagine the implications for this in organization. For example, what if Leadership is not, as we have thought for the past several centuries, about a particular way in which a person interacts/transacts with others, but rather the thing that emerges when two or more human beings are in a certain kind of relationship with each other. What are the implications for how we develop Leadership in our organizations?

What are the implications of this line of thinking for how you approach the marketplace?

The world is messy, complex, and unpredictable

What if you let go of the assumption that cause and effect were possible to understand? What if instead you proceeded from the understanding that every important thing that you do in your organization is a unique act (it's never been done by this particular group of people with these exact market conditions, etc.) and therefore, by it's nature, is a complex and unpredictable undertaking? What would you do differently? What role would relationship, conversation and trust have?

Control and predictability are possible and desirable

This is a cousin of the last assumption. Like cause and effect, if we didn't fundamentally assume that everything –and everyone - could ultimately be controlled and be made to be predictable, much of what we do in industrial organizations would make no sense.

Resources are finite and must be used efficiently

A 'resource' by its nature is something that is used – and something that is eventually used up. So the resources that are most central to our business are the ones that we compete aggressively for and, when we have them, attempt to squeeze every last bit of energy out of. Our whole mindset is that we must USE the resource before it disappears.

The most important manifestation of this to look at is the Human Resource. No matter how genuinely we may care about the people who work for us, the design of the Industrial Era organization compels us to squeeze as much out of them as we can because they are a finite commodity. Perhaps your organization attempts to make them happy, fulfilled, etc. in the process – which is great – but note that the desired outcome is still to use that Resource as efficiently as possible while it's around.

There is always great opportunity in a breakdown

What if the world is truly complex and unpredictable and breakdowns are therefore very likely? What then? What would have to be different for you and your organization to operate from a mindset that jumps on breakdowns, not as a cause for redoubling control systems, but as an opportunity to create totally new value?

Source is infinite if you can tap into it

Consider that each human being carries 'Source'; that they have a unique set of commitments relative to which they are willing to make massive contributions. Does your organization allow individuals to be a Source of value versus a Resource that is used to create value? This is not wordplay. Consider the baristas at Starbucks versus the counter person at Dunkin' Donuts. The former has a great deal of space in which to generate unique value based upon their own Source and the needs of the customer in front of them; the latter is an employee, a Resource that is used for 8 hours a day to engage in a finite set of transactions with customers.

Now What!?

Whatever you found of value in this little book would benefit not from action, but from conversation. There are no doubt many things for you to do, but we have found that the most useful starting point is to use the distinctions in this book to create conversations with your peers and employees. Use these conversations to explore what is possible for you and to let a different vision of your organization and business emerge.

Here are some questions for you and your organization to consider:

What are your biggest organizational concerns and how can those concerns be reframed based upon the distinctions the Triple-Soy Decaf-Latte Era?

What would happen if you let go of the assumption that you can control your message in the marketplace? What new possibilities would exist for you if this were the case? How would you measure success in such a world? What aspects of your current reality would you have to reframe? What would this do to your identity as a Marketing professional? What would your job now be?

What would happen if you let go of the assumption that it is valuable to control and predict the behavior of people within the organization? What new possibilities would exist for your organization if this were the case? How would you measure success in such a world? What aspects of your current reality would you have to reframe? What would this do to your identity as a Manager? What would your job now be?

How do you measure the state of your organization's relationships? Odds are, most of these metrics relate to short-term or long-term transactions. What if you considered the relationship itself as the outcome of your business, the end goal (versus the transactions that ensue from the relationships); what would you now measure? How would this reframing inform how your business is organized? What does the leader's role now become?

What conversations do you actively or passively inhibit within your organization? What blind spots do your organizational vision, mission, goals and policies create; in what ways do they inhibit employee contribution and innovation? Are your employees active, self-generating members of a high-accountability and high-autonomy 'cell' within your organization or are they role-based performers responsible for the execution of a discreet set of transactions?

Most organizations are designed to focus on tangible drivers of value (transaction volume, revenue, productivity, etc.). With how much rigor does your organization currently pay attention to intangible drivers of value (e.g., social capital, trust, conversation)? What risk does this introduce? Consider the possibility that tangible drivers are the by-products of intangible drivers. How would this inform what you emphasize within your organization and marketplace? What would you need to redesign in your organizational and marketplace strategies?

What are the attributes of the organization that would put your company (or some part of your company) out of business virtually overnight? What is it that you fail to deliver for employees and/or customers that, if someone else could, would cause your employees/customers to leave you? If your response includes only tangible items (better price, higher salary, etc.), you're not looking deeply enough.

Center for Leadership Studies

www.centerforleadershipstudies.com

Our transformed marketplace is forcing a shift from the veneration of corporate predictability as the creator of value to an appreciation of a deliberately fluid environment as this century's generator of innovation and competitive advantage. This fundamental change in orientation requires a corresponding evolution in leaders and leadership.

The Center for Leadership Studies is at the forefront of this transformation, providing the fundamental tools of personal and organizational development - methodology training, expert consulting and content exploration – from the perspective of the new corporate reality: successful leaders in the 21st century will not control, they will allow.

Mel Toomey
Principal & Managing Partner
CLS Degree & Certification Programs

Alpesh Bhatt
Principal & Managing Partner
CLS Advisory & Dialogue Services

Brent Robertson
Practitioner
CLS Advisory & Dialogue Services

Made in the USA
Lexington, KY
25 February 2014